信仰影响生活

Social Emotional and Multicultural Learning |
Non-Fiction Series

Copyright © 2022 by Level Learning, INC. and Washington Yu Ying PCS™
Original and Edited Text Copyright © 2022 by Washington Yu Ying PCS™

All rights reserved. No part of this book in whole or part may be reproduced without written permission from the publisher.

Published by Level Learning, INC.
Content Contributors:
Washington Yu Ying PCS™ - Shuo Li, Pearl Zao He You
Level Learning - Jingyao Qi

Illustrations by: Matt Austin

Leveling classification based on Level Learning standard.
For full description, visit www.levellearning.com

ISBN 978-1-64040-090-0
Simplified Chinese Edition

About Level Learning:

Level Learning provides a literacy focused curriculum specifically designed for K-12 Chinese as a Second Language classrooms. Our program offers 20 levels of specific and detailed objectives, leveled texts and passages, mastery-based online assessment, and analytics to enable data-driven instruction. Level Learning reading curriculum for both literature and informational text emphasize grammar and comprehension skills to help teachers develop confident and independent Chinese language readers. The non-fiction series of books are specifically designed to support our informational text course based on multiple national standards. To learn more about our entire offering, visit www.levellearning.com.

About Washington Yu Ying PCS™:

Washington Yu Ying PCS is a Mandarin English dual language immersion International Baccalaureate (IB) World school. Yu Ying's mission is to inspire and prepare young people to create a better world by challenging them to reach their full potential in a nurturing Chinese/English educational environment. Yu Ying's comprehensive IB, dual immersion curriculum equips students with global competencies for success in the real world. As a leader in immersion education, Yu Ying is determined to advance Chinese language programs and global citizenry education by helping other schools create and strengthen their Chinese programs. For more information, email: products@washingtonyuying.org

世界上有很多不同的宗教信仰，基督教、佛教、伊斯兰教和犹太教是信仰人数众多的几大宗教。不同宗教信仰的人，他们的生活方式也有很大不同。

信仰不同的人会庆祝不一样的节日。基督徒会庆祝圣诞节；犹太教徒会庆祝"光明节"；而信仰伊斯兰教的穆斯林会用一整月的时间来庆祝"斋月"。

除了节日以外,信仰对人们的生活还有什么影响呢?不知道你有没有发现,不同信仰的人,饮食习惯也不太一样。

有些你认为美味可口的食物，对于其他人来说可能是一种禁忌！犹太教徒和穆斯林都不吃猪肉，而有些佛教徒则完全不吃肉。所以，和朋友聚会的时候，我们不仅要考虑朋友们的口味，也要考虑到他们的信仰和饮食习惯。

不同的信仰有不同的结婚仪式。比如：犹太新郎在婚礼结束前要用脚踏碎一个玻璃杯子；在中东伊斯兰教的穆斯林婚礼上，新娘会在手和手臂上画上精美的图案；而在基督教的婚礼上，新郎和新娘则需要宣读誓言。

虽然不同宗教信仰的人会庆祝不同的节日，有不同的饮食习惯和婚礼仪式，但是这些宗教信仰都鼓励人们做诚实、善良的人。

不同的信仰形成了不同的文化和风俗，影响着人们的思想和生活。了解不同的宗教信仰可以帮助我们更好地尊重他人和与他人相处。

Glossary

	Pinyin	English Definition
宗教	zōng jiào	religion
信仰	xìn yǎng	belief system
基督教	jī dū jiào	Christianity
佛教	fó jiào	Buddism
伊斯兰教	yī sī lán jiào	Islam
犹太教	yóu tài jiào	Judism
庆祝	qìng zhù	to celebrate
光明节	guāng míng jié	Hanukkah
穆斯林	mù sī lín	Muslim
斋月	zhāi yuè	Ramadan
除了	chú le	besides
以外	yǐ wài	apart from
还	hái	also
影响	yǐng xiǎng	affect
饮食习惯	yǐn shí xí guàn	eating habit

	Pinyin	English Definition
美味可口	měi wèi kě kǒu	tasty
禁忌	jìn jì	ban
猪肉	zhū ròu	pork
考虑	kǎo lǜ	to consider
口味	kǒu wèi	taste
结婚	jié hūn	marriage
仪式	yí shì	ceremony
婚礼	hūn lǐ	wedding
结束	jié shù	end
踏	tà	to step on
碎	suì	to break into pieces
玻璃	bō li	glass
中东	zhōng dōng	Middle East
手臂	shǒu bì	arm
精美	jīng měi	exquisite

Glossary

	Pinyin	English Definition
图案	tú àn	design
宣读	xuān dú	to read out
誓言	shì yán	oath
鼓励	gǔ lì	to encourage
诚实	chéng shí	honest
善良	shàn liáng	good deeds
文化	wén huà	culture
风俗	fēng sú	custom
尊重	zūn zhòng	respect
相处	xiāng chǔ	to get along

www.ingramcontent.com/pod-product-compliance
Lightning Source LLC
Chambersburg PA
CBHW041224070526
44584CB00001B/82